Color For Thought

Written and illustrated by
fifth-grade students
of Coast Episcopal School in
Long Beach, Mississippi

Contents

Your red strawberry milkshake might contain, yes, bugs!

Cochineal (kŏch'ə-nēl'), a scaly, cactus-eating insect is used to produce reds such as scarlet and crimson. Cochineal is a red dyestuff consisting of the dried crushed bodies of female cochineal insects. The bugs are harvested by brushing them from cacti into bags. It takes 70,000 insects to make one pound of cochineal. It is used to dye fabrics. The bugs also give products such as drinks, jam and strawberry yogurt their bright red colors.

Both the dye and the insect are called "cochineal."

1 cactus + 1 cactus = 2 cacti

The crimson pulp of Pomegranate (pŏm´ grăn´ ĭt) fruit is used to make beverages red.

The tiny lac insect is harvested for shellac (a plastic like substance) and a red dye (used in India and other Asian countries). Today, the lac insect is harvested mostly for shellac. Lac means "hundred thousand." About 17,000 to 90,000 insects are needed to product one pound of shellac. Some candy products are coated with shellac to give it that yummy shine.

Native people extracted red pigments for dyeing from the brazilwood tree. This was centuries before Brazil was discovered by the Portuguese. Brazil comes from the Portuguese "terra do brasil," meaning land of brazilwood.

PIGMENT: A substance used to create color. In art, pigment is often mixed with water or oil to make paint.

Give that orange leaf a break!

Do trees work? Of course they do. To feed their shiny green leaves, trees use sunlight to turn water and carbon dioxide into sugar. That is hard work, and hardworking trees also need a break. When autumn comes, the trees take a break and stop producing chlorophyll (the green stuff). When that happens, the carotenoid (the orange color already in the leaves) can finally show through. We now see a glowing sea of yellows, sparkling oranges and warm browns.

You probably didn't know that tree leaves are really orange and during the growing season, the green pigment (chlorophyll) just covers the orange pigment (carotenoid)!

You'll see the best autumn colors in your garden when there's been:
• A warm wet spring
• A not too hot or dry summer
• A fall with many warm days and cool nights

Mushroom colors under our feet!

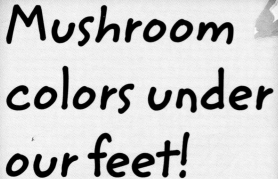

Color from mushrooms? Yes, a full color spectrum of dyes including bright red, yellow, orange and blue can be made from the wide variety of mushrooms available.

The dyes from mushrooms were originally used to color yarn and fabrics. It was later discovered that the residue from this dyeing process could be recycled to make colored paper and pigments for watercolor paints.

There you have it: dyes, paper and pigment from mushrooms!

Residue: Anything that remains after the main part has been taken away.

Spectrum: The range of colors that is revealed when light shines through a prism or through drops of water as in a rainbow.

Bile yellow extracted from a fish

Using bile for its gold color was a Greek tradition. The Greeks wrote their gilded letters with it. Centuries later, people used tortoise bile and even gallstones as a source of yellow in paintings. These were later replaced with vegetable yellows.

Chemists of the Middle Ages left this golden yellow recipe for us:

Take the bile of a big fish and mix it on a marble stone. Add a little chalk and a little vinegar. Grind it on the marble to a workable consistency. Write whatever you please with this on parchment and let it dry.

BILE: A greenish-yellow liquid produced by the liver.

From flower to flavor and color in a dish

STIGMA

Saffron is a very expensive substance that comes from the dried stigma of the crocus flower. The flowers are picked by hand and harvested in less than twenty days. Saffron is used as a yellow colorant in sausages, margarine, butter, cheese and drinks. It is also used for flavor and coloring in ice cream, sauces and dressings. Try to find saffron on your local grocer's spice shelf.

The robes of some Buddhist monks of China are dyed with saffron.

STIGMA: The part of the flower where pollen is deposited.

A penny + vinegar = green

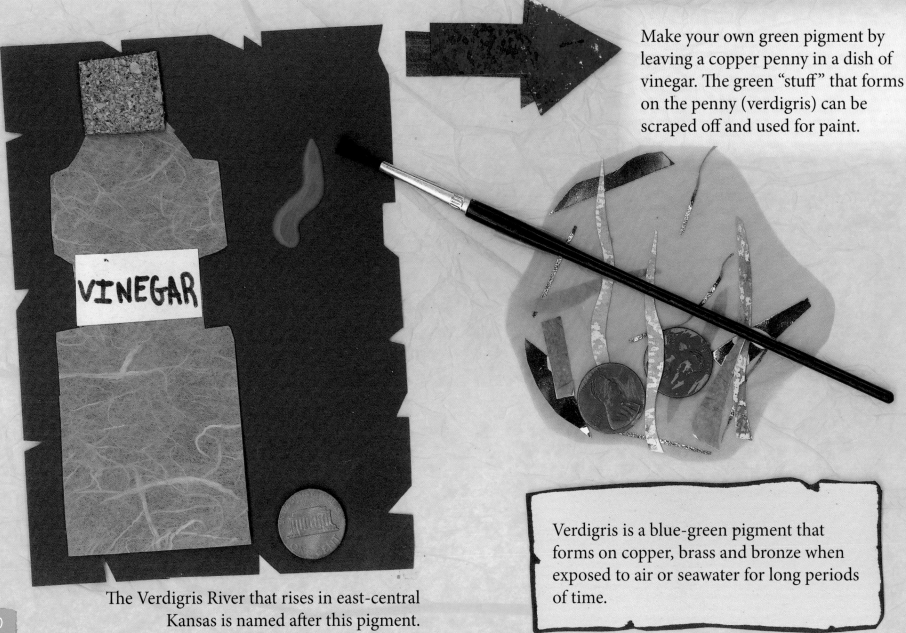

Make your own green pigment by leaving a copper penny in a dish of vinegar. The green "stuff" that forms on the penny (verdigris) can be scraped off and used for paint.

VINEGAR

The Verdigris River that rises in east-central Kansas is named after this pigment.

Verdigris is a blue-green pigment that forms on copper, brass and bronze when exposed to air or seawater for long periods of time.

Verdigris can form on copper pots used to cook acidic foods such as tomatoes.

Salt green was made like verdigris, but the copper plates were covered with honey and salt instead.

Emerald green is the most poisonous and dangerous of all pigments. It comes from basic copper arsenate.

The copper colors of the old works of art look like coarse splintered glass under a microscope while modern colors look mud-like under a microscope.

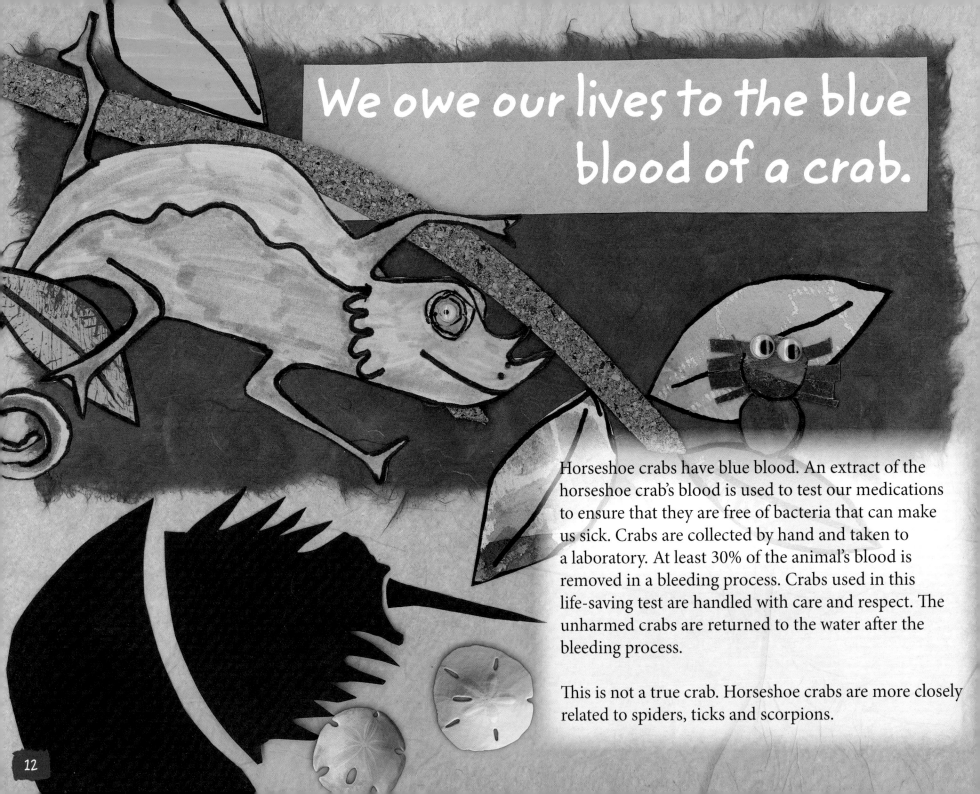

We owe our lives to the blue blood of a crab.

Horseshoe crabs have blue blood. An extract of the horseshoe crab's blood is used to test our medications to ensure that they are free of bacteria that can make us sick. Crabs are collected by hand and taken to a laboratory. At least 30% of the animal's blood is removed in a bleeding process. Crabs used in this life-saving test are handled with care and respect. The unharmed crabs are returned to the water after the bleeding process.

This is not a true crab. Horseshoe crabs are more closely related to spiders, ticks and scorpions.

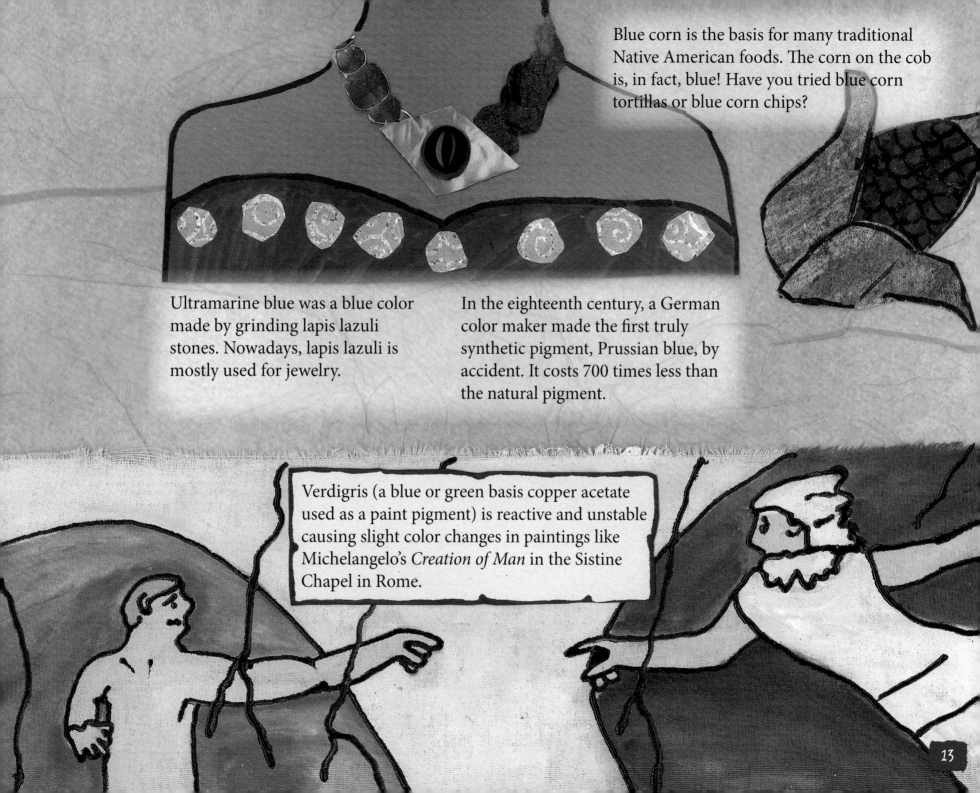

Blue corn is the basis for many traditional Native American foods. The corn on the cob is, in fact, blue! Have you tried blue corn tortillas or blue corn chips?

Ultramarine blue was a blue color made by grinding lapis lazuli stones. Nowadays, lapis lazuli is mostly used for jewelry.

In the eighteenth century, a German color maker made the first truly synthetic pigment, Prussian blue, by accident. It costs 700 times less than the natural pigment.

Verdigris (a blue or green basis copper acetate used as a paint pigment) is reactive and unstable causing slight color changes in paintings like Michelangelo's *Creation of Man* in the Sistine Chapel in Rome.

Prestigious and pricey purple from a snail

In ancient times, the source of purple was a closely guarded secret.

The Roman Emperor Aurelian refused to allow his wife to buy a purple-dyed silk dress because it cost its weight in gold.

Purple dye was produced from the murex. Murexes are sea snails with rough, spiny shells. They are common in warm seas. Many of them produce a yellow fluid that turns red or purple in sunlight. It took 12,000 shellfish to extract 1.5 grams of royal purple dye!

Animal-based colors from insects and snails were mentioned in the Bible for use in decorating temples.

While searching for a cure for malaria, William Perkin discovered a synthetic purple dye, mauve. He became a very rich man.

Synthetic: Man-made.

Malaria: An infectious disease transmitted by the bite of a female mosquito.

The Mardi Gras colors are purple, green and gold. Purple symbolizes justice, green is for faith and gold is for power.

Mardi Gras: A carnival period celebrated with parades and festivities.

Paint with sunscreen and shells

In Japan, oyster shells are aged for at least 20 years before they get crushed. The white pigment is then used to paint the faces of Japanese dolls.

Lead white was a very common pigment in the sixteenth century. It was manufactured from metal and shows up clearly on x-rays. Lead is a poison.

Lead white was replaced by zinc white because it was non-toxic and cheaper to produce. Zinc white is also known as Chinese white. Since ancient times, zinc has been known as a medicinal ointment. (That's also the white stuff you put on your nose to block out the sun.)

Organic: A product grown without the use of chemicals.

Toxic: Poisonous.

White cotton to dye for!

If you thought that cotton has always been white, read this. Native white, green, pink, lavender, yellow, red and brown colored cottons have been cultivated and spun for thousands of years.

These cotton fibers are naturally colorful when the ball opens in the field.

Modern textile processing prefers white cotton. White cotton is treated with pesticides and bleaches making it the most pesticide intensive crop grown in the USA. For every organic T-shirt and pair of jeans you buy, you save our planet from a pound of pesticides.

To grow enough cotton for one white T-shirt, you'll use approximately one-third of a pound of chemicals.

Colorful cotton is an organically produced product.

Ancient travelers to India told of the "vegetable lamb" – part animal, part plant – which grew on a plant and ate the grass around it. Beautiful cotton cloth was said to be woven from the fleeces of these "vegetable lambs" (known today as cotton balls).

Bountiful black has a beamy track!

Add a few drops of water. Mix until you have a thin ink.

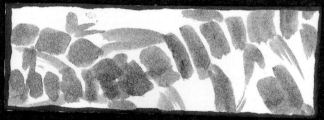

Hold the back of a small stoneware plate in the flame of a burning candle until black soot forms.

Carefully scrape the soot into a small cup. Add two drops of white multi-purpose glue to the soot. Mix it well.

Paint away!

Lamp black was popular in the Middle Ages. Soot was formed on a cold surface, like a plate, by passing a flame beneath it. The soot was collected and mixed with gum water to make India ink. This pigment is permanent. The Chinese use this ink for brush writing and painting on very absorbent surfaces. This was never used in history as a painting pigment.

18

Ivory black and bone black were both made from charred animal bones, tusks, and horns.

The Japanese make an inky black color from the soot and pitch of burned pine trees.

Kohl is a black make-up pencil that women in India use to outline the rims of their eyelids.

Graphite is a natural mineral but can be made artificially. The Greek word means "to write." Natural graphite has a greasy texture. It was used in mural paintings. When dry, it can be rubbed to glow like metal. In the Middle Ages, it was only used for drawing, not writing. It is very toxic and had to be sealed. The pencil you use at school is graphite compressed with fine clay.

Henna (hăn´-a) comes from the dried, ground leaves of a small shrub that grows in the East Indies, Arabia, Iran and North Africa. The dye varies from orange-red to brown. Henna is the oldest hair conditioner and hair dye. Cleopatra used it. Pharaohs' hands and feet were first dipped in henna before mummification. In Asia, women use henna to color their fingertips, nails and parts of their feet. Drawing on the skin with henna paste has become a fun craft to create non-permanent tattoos.

HENNA TATTOOS

Brown has been obtained from earth, shrubs and even... mummies!

The brown pigment used by European artists in many masterpieces was obtained by grinding the remains of Egyptian mummies.

Cheap browns, reds and yellows are found in soil and clay of different colors. Examples of the use of these can be seen in cave paintings.

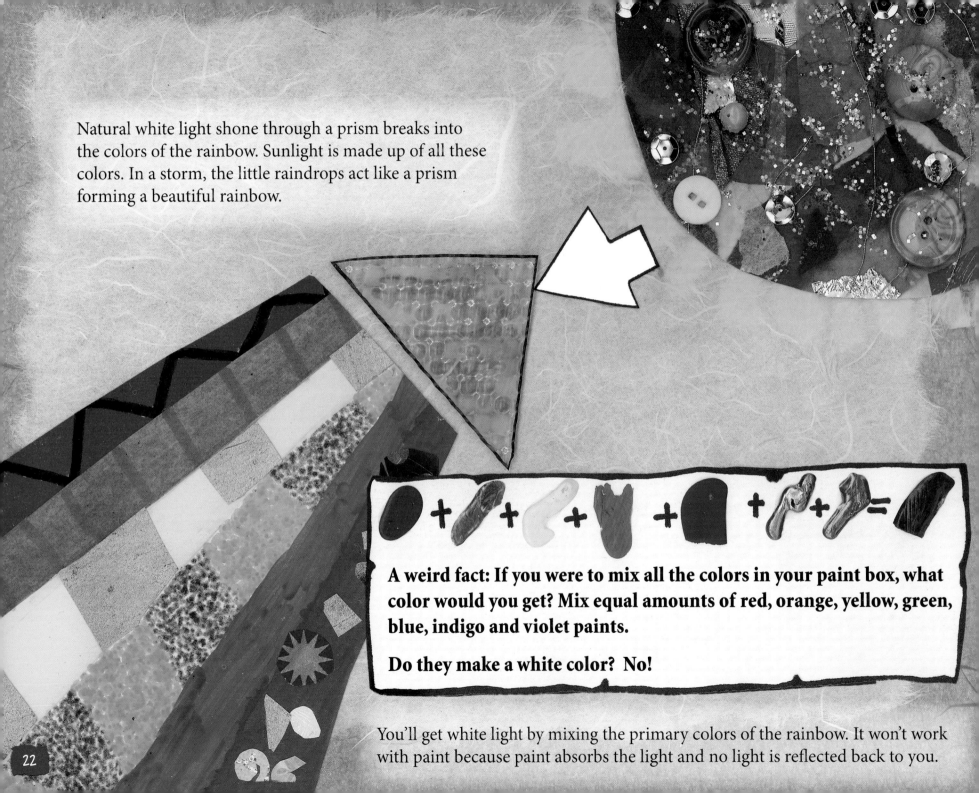

Natural white light shone through a prism breaks into the colors of the rainbow. Sunlight is made up of all these colors. In a storm, the little raindrops act like a prism forming a beautiful rainbow.

A weird fact: If you were to mix all the colors in your paint box, what color would you get? Mix equal amounts of red, orange, yellow, green, blue, indigo and violet paints.

Do they make a white color? No!

You'll get white light by mixing the primary colors of the rainbow. It won't work with paint because paint absorbs the light and no light is reflected back to you.

Making rainbows and loving it!

Fill a glass with water.

Balance the glass on the edge of a table so that the sun shines directly through the water onto the sheet of paper on the floor.

Adjust the glass and the paper until a rainbow forms on the paper.

The glass of water acts as a prism and as the white light passes through the water, it is broken up into the colors seen in a rainbow. Use this acronym (a word formed from the first letters of a series of words) to remember the order of the colors of the rainbow.

ROY G. BIV = red, orange, yellow, green, blue, indigo, violet
Acronym: A word formed from the first letters of a series of words.

START

1

2

3 It's autumn. Without the green chlorophyll, the orange pigment in the leaves can finally show. Skip a turn to admire the colors.

4

5

6

7 Congratulations! You tried making your own black ink and it actually worked! Change places with anyone else on the board!

8

9

10

11 In order to obtain a white pigment, you have to wait 20 years for your oyster shells to age. Skip a turn.

12

13

14 The crushed remains of mummies have been used as brown pigment in paintings. Will your friends believe you? Move forward 3 spaces.

15

16

17

18

19

20

21

22 Thanks to Roy G. Biv, you remember the order of the colors of the rainbow. Move forward 2 spaces.

23

24

25

26

27 You have just landed a summer job painting Henna tattoos at the beach. Move forward 6 spaces.

28

29 You volunteer to work on an organic cotton farm. Go forward 9 spaces to start picking colorful cotton.

Our chameleon is hungry!
Help him get to the fly.
Use a die and coins as play pieces.
Have fun!
(1 die + 1 die = 2 dice)

41

42

43

44 Forgot to wear purple to the Mardi Gras parade? Move back 6 spaces.

45

46

47

48

49

40 You start a program to make people aware of the value of the blue blood of the horseshoe crab. Move forward 8 spaces.

39

38

50 Being a vegetarian, you are disgusted to find that bugs are used to color some foods red but then again, it could have been worse. Move forward 4 spaces.

37 You stay behind to harvest saffron to dye your robe yellow. Skip a turn.

51

55 You got sunburned. Stay inside for a while. Move back 4 spaces.

54

53

52

57

56

36

31

35

58 You made colored paper using mushroom dye residue. Move forward 3 spaces.

32

33

34

59

60 The copper penny you wanted to use to make verdigris green is missing. Go back 10 spaces.

➤ You did it!

Get your facts straight!

Chameleons can't turn polka-dotted, bright orange or even plaid!
Most chameleons can only change to green, brown or gray.
Chameleons usually change color to blend with their surroundings.
Each species of chameleon has its own color range.

Why do chameleons change color?

Light: Light reflecting off of them changes their color.
Temperature: They can make themselves flat and dark to absorb more heat.
Mood: During mating or when threatened, a chameleon will change color.
Health: A sick chameleon will stay pale because it doesn't have the energy to change color.

How do they do it?

Beneath the chameleon's transparent skin are many cell layers that contain pigments. Chameleons change their color by opening and closing these cells. The pigments reflect light in different colors.

Can you think of other animals that can change color?

Color for thought...

You also have pigments which cause your skin to darken in the sun.

Even though our skin is our body's biggest organ, people don't always take care of it. In small doses, the sun is good for us but overexposure to the sun can cause permanent damage to our skin.

Think about it...

Slap on your sunscreen, get that funky hat and put on those goofy sunglasses before you hit the beach. At least you won't look like beef jerky in 20 years!

What's your color?

People have 99% of the same DNA. Less than 1% determines the color of our skin... so we are all more alike than different!

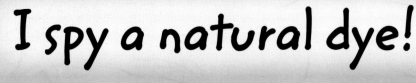

I spy a natural dye!

Let's dye eggs! This can get messy!!

Wear old clothes and cover your work area with plastic. (A black garbage bag would do.)
Be sure to ask parent permission before beginning this project.
Ask an adult to help you boil the eggs and the dyes.

Step 1: Wash eggs well before dyeing.

Step 2: Boil the eggs for 10 minutes.

Use any one or all of these natural ingredients to make your dyes.

The more of the natural ingredient you use and the longer the egg soaks (maybe overnight), the darker the color.

Blue: Boil sliced red cabbage for 30 minutes. This dye looks purple but will dye eggs blue. Cabbage dye only works when it has cooled down.

Pale Green: Boil spinach leaves.

Beige Brown: One tablespoon of coffee plus ½ a teaspoon of vinegar dissolved in a cup of water.

Reddish Brown: Boil four cups of onion skins for 30 minutes.

Yellow: Add one tablespoon of ground turmeric and one tablespoon of vinegar to water.

Pink: The juice from pickled beets.

Experiment with some natural ingredients of your own.
You'll impress all your friends and teachers with your colorful eggs!

Get creative with an eggshell mosaic!

After eating your eggs, you can make great pictures. Just keep all the shells. Glue the pretty eggshells down to form a work of art.

Index

Bibliography

(Where we found our facts)

Frayling, Christopher and Helen, and Ron van der Meer. *The Art Pack*. Aldred A. Knopf, Inc. 1992

Color. Scholastic Inc., 1997 pp 8, 9, 18, 26

Siegel, Alice and McLoone, Margo. *Kid's Almanac of Geography*. Blackbirch Press, Inc. 2000 Pp 22-123.

The American Heritage Dictionary of the English Language. American Heritage Publishing Company, Inc. and Houghton Mifflin Company. 1969.

Williams, Helen. *Stories in Art*. The Millbrook Press. 1992 pp.31

Hammond Winifred. *Cotton From Farm to Market*. Coward-McCann, Inc. 1968. pp 78-79

Richardson, Joy. *Looking at Pictures*. National Gallery Publications Limited. 1997. pp 28, 38, 40

Arora, David. *Mushrooms Demystified*. Ten Speed Press. 1986. pp. 418, 455, 712.

This class obtained information for this book from the following websites, during the 2002-2003 school year. Websites change over time, and the information on these sites may change or no longer be available in the future. Parents and teachers should check these sites prior to future access by children.

www.geocities.com/mkatz925/nytsaffron.htm

www.jcsparks.com/painted/pigment_print.html

www.horseshoecrab.org/med/med.html

www.cahe.nmsu.edu/pubs/_h/h-226.html

www.pffc-online.com/ar/paper_history_shellfish_royalty/

www.athenmills.com/benefits_of_organic.htm

www.athenmills.com/fox_fibre.htm

www.webexhibits.org/pigments/indiv/history/zincwhite.html

www.webexhibits.org/pigments/indiv/color/reds.html

www.lanakids.com/sun.html

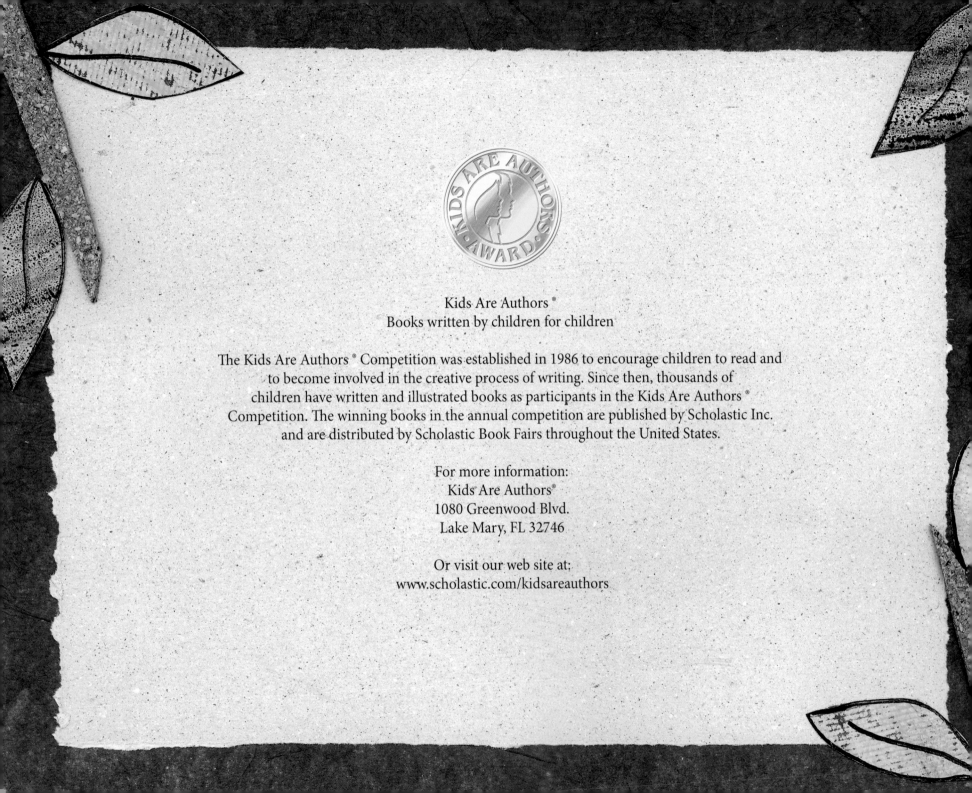

Kids Are Authors®
Books written by children for children

The Kids Are Authors® Competition was established in 1986 to encourage children to read and
to become involved in the creative process of writing. Since then, thousands of
children have written and illustrated books as participants in the Kids Are Authors®
Competition. The winning books in the annual competition are published by Scholastic Inc.
and are distributed by Scholastic Book Fairs throughout the United States.

For more information:
Kids Are Authors®
1080 Greenwood Blvd.
Lake Mary, FL 32746

Or visit our web site at:
www.scholastic.com/kidsareauthors